Fun with Action Rhymes and Poems

Brenda Williams

Brilliant Publications

Contents

Introduction 3
Theme Index 5
Teacher's Notes 9
Early Learning Goals Summary Chart 23
Action Rhymes and Poems 26
Title index 108

Acknowledgements

The following poems and action rhymes were first published by:

Scholastic Ltd
Apple Bobbing (1999)
Caterpillar, Caterpillar (1998)
Colours Here, and Colours There (2001)
Countd own to Bedtime (2001)
Dear Potato (2002)
Drawing Shapes (2001)
Finger Teddies (1999)
I've Made a Star (1999)
I Can Do Opposites (1999)
I Have a Baby Sister (2001)
Jack Frost (2001)
Just a Taste (2000)
Look at Shapes (2001)
Magic Carpet (2002)
Make the Bed (1998)
My House (2001)
New Life (2000)
Over the Sea (2000)
Puddles (2002)
Scuttling Spider (1999)
Shape that Dough (2001)

Show Five Fingers (1998)
The Chip Shop Man (2002)
The Doctor (2002)
The Dragon Dance (2000)
The Horse Post (2002)
The Market (2000)
The Mehndi Tree (2002)
The Scarecrow (2001)
There Goes the Train (2002)
Twinkle, Twinkle Christmas Lights (2001)
When I Was Born (2001)
When Night Comes (2002)
When the Sun Steals Away (2000)
Who Am I? (2002)
Winter Weather (1999)

Oxford University Press
Gloves (2001)
The Train Journey (2001)

Practical Pre-School
Farmer, Farmer (2001)

Published by Brilliant Publications, 1 Church View, Sparrow Hall Farm, Edlesborough, Dunstable, Bedfordshire LU6 2ES

www.brilliantpublications.co.uk

Written by Brenda Williams
Illustrated by Angela Jolliffe

ISBN 1 903853 50 8

First published in the UK in 2004
10 9 8 7 6 5 4 3 2 1

© Brenda Williams

Introduction

All the action rhymes and peoms in this book have been written with the enjoyment of young children in mind. I have tried to capture for them the sense of fun, sharing, and togetherness I have experienced in their company whilst exploring poetry with them over many years. It is their delight in, and their responses to, rhythm and rhyme which have been my greatest source of inspiration.

Developing a Love of Rhythm and Rhyme

The youngest babies are comforted by the rise and fall of a familiar voice and soon make the connection between vocal sounds and facial expressions. As they seek to communicate, they begin to mimic both the sounds and the related expressions and go on to copy movements, such as clapping hands.

Even at an early stage of children's development, action rhymes and songs can further encourage them to link language with movement, reinforcing familiar words and developing new ones. But, what is equally important, poetry fosters a love of rhythm and rhyme which lays the foundations to an understanding of the patterns of language, mathematics and music.

Enjoying the fun of rhyme, hearing the sounds, fitting words to simple actions, and experiencing pace are important factors in creating a sense of beat and rhythm.

Children love learning rhymes, and soon establish favourites they ask to return to again and again. They find them easy to remember and retain because of the rhyming words and patterns. Participating in a group gives them a sense of sharing and belonging.

By introducing children to a love of poetry, we are leading them to a life-long fascination with the music of words, the power and influence of language in conjuring imagery and feelings, and a means of communicating in a structured but stimulating form.

Themes and Topics

Many early years' settings base their cross-curricular activities on a theme or topic which gives a focus and coherence to planned activities. This anthology is referenced under many of these favourite themes in order to provide practitioners with a quick and easy access to the kind of thematic rhyme they so often need. Further, to give greater versatility, the rhymes are linked and cross-referenced not only to other themes within the book, but also to other popular themes. (See Theme Index, page 5).

How the Rhymes and Poems Link to the Early Learning Goals

First and foremost, the rhymes are for children to enjoy! Listening and responding to the rhymes, and sharing the fun of them as an activity in its own right are more than sufficient justification for using them in an early years setting. Many practitioners will find this collection useful just to dip into at different times of the day, knowing that children will benefit from the three 'Rs' of rhythm, rhyme and repetition. Some of the action rhymes will provide a means of releasing energy, while others will help create a sense of calmness.

Poems and action rhymes can, however, also provide an informal and easy way to introduce new ideas or topics for discussion, and can encourage humour, prediction, role play and imagination. One of the intentions of the book is to provide rhymes which have relevance to children in today's world, and this makes them particularly suitable for opening up other areas of learning.

The notes give suggestions on using the rhymes to support learning at the Foundation Stage. The content and theme of each rhyme give rise to an activity which is in line with one of the six areas of learning covered by the Early Learning Goals. Between them the activities provide full coverage of the Foundation Stage curriculum. An overall view of the balance of activities is given in the chart on pages 23–25.

Many of the rhymes can, of course, be adapted to support other activities and it is hoped that practitioners will use the suggestions here as a starting point for their own ideas.

Theme Index

Theme and Rhymes	Page	Links to Themes Within this Book	Links to Other Popular Themes
All About Me			
I Can Do Opposites	26	Changes	Opposites
			Things I Can Do
My Hands, My Feet	27		Things I Can Do
Show Five Fingers	28	Counting Rhymes	
Gloves	29	Counting Rhymes	Clothes
I Can Make Noises	30		Things I Can Do
			Sounds
Animals and Mini-Beasts			
Just a Taste?	31	All About Me (senses)	Senses
Rapping in the Jungle	32		Music, Rhythm and Beat
Finger Farm	33	Counting Rhymes	Farms
Spider, Spider, Spinning Well	34	Homes	
Jungle Wood	35	Homes	Woods
Mini-beasts	36	Homes	Woods
Changes			
Caterpillar, Caterpillar	37	Animals and Mini-beasts	Growth
All Is Quiet	38		Sounds
Clouds	39	Weather	In the Air
Changing Sands	40	Seasons	
When I Was Born	41	All About Me	Growth
Colours			
Let's Climb up a Rainbow	42	Weather	Water
The Mehndi Tree	43	Festivals	Celebrations and Traditions
			Patterns
Painting Pictures	44	Changes	Things I Can Do
Colours Here and Colours There	45		Out and About
Counting Rhymes			
Finger Teddies	46	Special Things	Toys
			Bears
Down in the Jungle	47	Animals and Mini-beasts	Jungles
One Little Monkey	48	Animals and Mini-beasts	Jungles
Countdown to Bedtime	49	Family	
		Day and Night	

Day and Night

About Time!	50	All About Me	Time
Stepping Through the Day	51	Counting Rhymes	My Day
When the Sun Steals Away	52		In the Air
When Night Comes	53		Light and Dark
			Reflections
Day and Night	54		Opposites

Family

Family Barbecue	55	Counting Rhymes	
		People	
		Food and Shopping	
		Seasons	
Over the Sea	56	Journeys	The Sea
Family Lunch	57	Counting Rhymes	
		Food and Shopping	
I Have a Baby Sister	58	All About Me	New Life
			Growth
Am I the Tallest?	59		Measurement
			Growth

Festivals

Eid Mubarak (Happy Eid)	60	Day and Night	Holidays
Candles for Hanukkah	61	Counting Rhymes	Light and Dark
I've Made a Star	62	Seasons	Christmas
The Dragon Dance	63	Colours	New Year
		Animals	Story and Fantasy
Apple Bobbing	64	Seasons	Autumn
		Food and Shopping	

Food and Shopping

The Market	65		Places Around Us
			Where We Live
I'm the Butcher	66	People	Places Around Us
			Where We Live
			Clothes for the Job
I Love Bread	67	All About Me	Nonsense Rhymes
Chocolate	68	All About Me	Things I like
A Fruit to Suit?	69		Clothes
Dear Potato	70	All About Me	

Homes

Scuttling Spider	71	Animals and Mini-beasts	
In Granny's Garden	72	People	Fantasy Homes
My House	73	All About Me	
Make the Bed	74		

Journeys

The Train Journey	75		Transport
			Fast and Slow
Farm Journey	76	Animals and Mini-beasts	Farms
Travelling	77		Transport
			Fast and Slow
Magic Carpet	78	Food and Shopping	Story and Fantasy
There Goes the Train	79		Transport
			Town and Country

People

The Doctor	80	All About Me	
Farmer, Farmer	81	Food and Shopping	Farms
			Autumn
			Harvest
			Transport
Who Am I?	82	Journeys	Where We Live
The Chip Shop Man	83	Food and Shopping	Where We Live

Seasons

Patterns on the Sand	84	Shapes	Patterns
		Special Things	Seaside
The Scarecrow	85		Birds
			Farms
			Clothes
Autumn's Here!	86	Animals and Mini-beasts	
		Weather	
New Life	87	Animals and Mini-beasts	New Life
			Farms
Jack Frost	88	Shapes	Patterns
		Weather	

Shapes

Look at Shapes	89	All About Me	
Shape that Dough	90	Changes	
Night and Day Shapes	91	Day and Night	Opposites
			In the Air
Drawing Shapes	92		Patterns

Songs and Games

Sailing on the Ocean	93	Journeys	The Sea
			Transport
Twinkle, Twinkle, Christmas Lights	94	Festivals	Nonsense Rhymes
		Seasons	Christmas
Here's a Toy Box	95	Special Things	Toys
The Horse Post	96	Journeys	Transport
			Long Ago
Spider, Spider	97	Animals and Mini-beasts	
		Homes	
Dawdling Dinosaurs	98	Animals and Mini-beasts	Long Ago
			Dinosaurs

Special Things

My Bear	99	All About Me	Toys
			Bears
			Friends
These Are My Special Things	100	All About Me	
My Tiny Treasures	101	All About Me	Collections
My Grandma	102	Family	
		People	

Weather

Rainbow, Rainbow	103	Colours	Patterns
		Seasons	Water
Winter Weather	104	Seasons	
The Wind Wizard	105	Seasons	In the Air
A Puddleful of Raindrops	106	Seasons	
Puddles	107	Seasons	Water
			Reflections

Teacher's Notes
Using the Rhymes to Achieve the Early Learning Goals

All About Me

I Can Do Opposites (page 26)
Once they are familiar with this rhyme, encourage children to think about other ways they 'do' opposite words, such as picking up and putting down. Discuss times when they are happy or sad, and invite them to draw pictures of themselves with a smile and a frown.
CLL – *To explore the meanings of words.*

My Hands, My Feet (page 27)
Provide a range of different textures for children to touch, stroke and describe. Talk about the way they use their hands to hold, help and create. Encourage them to demonstrate how confident they are in using their feet in the ways described in the poem.
PD – *To move with confidence.*

Show Five Fingers (page 28)
Display six children's gloves and demonstrate how the number of fingers decreases in each verse of the rhyme. Help children make paper cut-outs of their hands, and fold fingers back to 'take them away'.
MD – *To begin to relate subtraction to 'taking away'.*

Gloves (page 29)
Invite children to put on and take off gloves, and discuss how difficult it can sometimes be. Show them how to turn gloves the right way round by looking at patterns and seams.
PSED – *To dress and undress independently.*

I Can Make Noises (page 30)
Discuss times when children want to make the sounds in the rhyme. Talk about their need to express happiness, sadness, boredom, illness and frustration. Explain how we should try to understand these needs in others.
PSED – *To express needs and feelings in appropriate ways.*

Animals and Mini-beasts

Just a Taste? (page 31)
Use a variety of fruit for children to sniff, touch, see and taste, and listen to other children describing their reactions. Discuss the kinds of food that the animals in the rhyme would usually eat.
PSED – *To understand that people and animals have different needs.*

Rapping in the Jungle (page 32)
Involve children in making large cut-out pictures of the animals in the rhyme, and display them in a jungle environment on the wall. Place a copy of the rhyme alongside. Encourage children to experiment with different beats on drums to match the rhythm of the poem.
CD – *To use imagination in art and design, music and role play.*

Finger Farm (page 33)
Invite some children to role play the characters in the poem, following each other in a procession. Use a large box with a cut-out door for the house, with one child hiding inside as Thumb-thumb.
CLL – *To listen with enjoyment and respond to rhymes and poems.*

Spider, Spider, Spinning Well (page 34)
Take children to see spider's webs in the environment. Look at pictures of spiders and webs. Discuss the way a spider spins its web, and how it catches its food. Make a giant spider from black sugar paper, and count its legs.
KUW – *To find out about and identify some features of living things.*

Jungle Wood (page 35)
Make cardboard spiders, snails and ants in large, medium and small sizes, and use them for sorting activities of both size and type. Place some of the ants in a 'long parade' numbered 1–9 and encourage children to count them.
MD – *To use the language of 'larger', 'smaller', 'the same' to describe size; to count reliably up to 10.*

Mini-beasts (page 36)
Take children on a walk through woods and lift stones, leaves and twigs. Encourage them to look carefully at insects they see underneath. Catch a few in a small plastic microscope to observe before returning them to the habitat.
KUW – *To observe, find out about and identify features of the natural world.*

Changes

Caterpillar, Caterpillar (page 37)
Roll 'caterpillars' from green Plasticine. Have some crawling up a twig placed in a plant pot, and display others crawling, and curled up tight. Provide collage materials and butterfly shapes for children to create their own butterflies.
CD – *To express and communicate ideas using a widening range of materials.*

All Is Quiet (page 38)
Follow the poem with a discussion about quiet and noisy times. For example, compare the quietness of a bedtime story with a noisy playtime. Involve children in drawing pictures with captions, and use these to create two group books, 'Quiet Times' and 'Noisy Times', which children can browse through.
CLL – *To use writing as a means of communicating ideas.*

Clouds (page 39)

Observe the weather over a few days, encouraging children to notice the colour and formation of clouds, and which ones bring about a change in the weather. Help them to explain those changes.

KUW – *To ask questions about why things happen.*

Changing Sands (page 40)

Use the poem to encourage children to think about other things they can change using their hands, small tools and paints etc. Involve them in activities such as building with bricks and construction sets, baking cakes, moulding Plasticine, painting pictures and changing colours.

PD – *To handle tools, objects, construction and malleable materials with increasing control.*

When I Was Born (page 41)

Invite children to demonstrate some of the things they can do mentioned in the poem. Set up equipment for them to travel around, under, over, and through, climb up on, jump down from, and balance on. Encourage them to learn something new, such as catching or throwing a bean bag.

PD – *To travel around, under, over and through equipment and to develop co-ordination.*

Colours

Let's Climb up a Rainbow (page 42)

Invite children to paint rainbows in red, yellow and blue. Show them how to mix yellow and blue paint to make green, before adding it to their rainbow. Ask them to suggest other colours and experiment with mixing them.

CD – *To explore colour in two dimensions.*

The Mehndi Tree (page 43)

Help children to draw and cut out shapes of their own hands, then involve them in creating their own patterns and designs on the cut-outs using coloured felt pens.

CD – *To use their imagination in art and design.*

Painting Pictures (page 44)

Make a simple bar chart of the colours mentioned in the poem. Fill a square in the appropriate column and colour for each thing the children suggest. For example, 'Snow is white.' Compare the differences in the columns as they grow, using the words 'more' and 'less'.

MD – *To use language such as 'more' or 'less' to compare two quantities.*

Colours Here and Colours There (page 45)

Help children to understand that this is a list poem. Talk about other lists, such as shopping lists, and lists of names. In a group of five, ask each child to say a colour, and list these on a flip chart. Then ask them to suggest something to add to each colour listed, for example 'yellow banana'.

CLL – *To attempt writing in different forms e.g. lists.*

Counting Rhymes

Finger Teddies (page 46)
Make some cardboard teddies and stand or hang them in a row. Invite younger children to count them with you as you touch each teddy. Add numbers 1–5 to the teddies for use with older children, inviting them to point out different teddies by their number.

MD – *To willingly attempt to count in the correct order. To recognize numerals 1–5.*

Down in the Jungle (page 47)
Use the rhyme as an introduction to collecting other sets of three. For example, farm animals, toy cars, beads, pencils. Involve children in finding three items and placing in groups.

MD – *To recognize groups with one, two or three objects.*

One Little Monkey (page 48)
Involve children in creating a large display tree at child's height and three cut-out monkeys. Stick one monkey on the tree using Blu-tack®, then invite a child to stick on another one. Discuss the relative positions of the monkeys using language such as 'higher', 'lower', 'the same'. Add another monkey and compare again.

MD – *To use everyday words to describe position.*

Countdown to Bedtime (page 49)
Invite children to talk to the group about their bedtime. Who usually puts them to bed? Who kisses them goodnight? Do they have special toys to cuddle?

PSED – *To talk freely about their home.*

Day and Night

About Time! (page 50)
Suggest that children think about their routine in the morning. Write down some of their ideas on a flip chart, and read them back to them. Together, work out a sequence to their routine, and write a group poem in a similar form to this rhyme, starting with something like 'It's ... opening up my eyes time, getting out of bed time,' etc.

CLL – *To listen with enjoyment to rhymes and make up their own.*

Stepping Through the Day (page 51)
Ask children to role play the day suggested in the rhyme by improvising with available equipment. Take photographs – ideally with a digital camera to use in conjunction with a computer. Display the photographs or prints with the relevant lines from the poem. Discuss the way the camera/computer has helped the children to record the day.

KUW – *To use information and communication technology to support their learning.*

When the Sun Steals Away (page 52)
Make a simple tabard for each child, one in blue sugar paper and the others in black. Help children to draw round templates and cut out one large yellow sun, a large silver moon and several silver stars, and glue to the tabards appropriately. Make up basic forward, backward and sideways movements to suitable music for children to create a dance to the poem.
PD – *To handle tools and objects with increasing control. To move with imagination.*

When Night Comes (page 53)
Choose a dark day to carry out simple experiments of light and dark: switching on and off the lights, lighting candles, and using torches. Open up a torch and show children the bulb, battery, connecting strip, and switch, and explain how it works.
KUW – *To ask questions about why things happen and how things work.*

Day and Night (page 54)
Make two wall displays representing day and night, involving the children in a variety of activities using a range of materials for drawing, painting and collage to create the ideas mentioned in the rhyme.
CD – *To work creatively on a large or small scale.*

Family

Family Barbecue (page 55)
Invite children to talk to the group about who would come to a family party at their house. Ask them to draw a picture of themselves and their family, and to point out different people at their party.
PSED – *To show a strong sense of self as a member of their family.*

Over the Sea (page 56)
Discuss different ways the children may travel to visit members of their family. Do they go by boat or plane 'over the sea', or by car, train, bus or foot to see them? In a large space, ask children to invent ways to imitate these different ways of travelling, for example pretending to row a boat, flying with arms outstretched, forming a line to create a train. Invite them to move around the space, quickly then slowly, without bumping into each other.
PD – *To show awareness of space, of themselves and of others.*

Family Lunch (page 57)
Ask individual children to use plastic plates and cutlery to set the table for up to five people. Help them count out the plates and put them in place, and then count out the cutlery. With more able children suggest that more people arrive unexpectedly and ask how many more plates etc. they will need. Then count how many plates are needed altogether.
MD – *To count out up to six objects from a larger group. To use developing mathematical skills to solve practical problems.*

A Fruit to Suit? (page 69)
Bring in as many of the fruits mentioned in the poem as possible, and discuss what is meant by a 'yellow zip-off suit', the strawberry's 'hat', and the plum's 'dress of velveteen'. Invite children to touch and taste the fruit and express their likes and dislikes. Talk to them about the importance of fruit to keep healthy.
PD – *To recognize the importance of keeping healthy and those things which contribute to this.*

Dear Potato (page 70)
Hand round a real, large potato and talk about how it looks and feels. Encourage children to express their opinions about the different ways to enjoy potatoes mentioned in the poem. Liaise with parents to arrange a 'potato party' day. Have chips delivered, bake potatoes, or hand round crisps depending on children's tastes.
PSED – *To have a developing awareness of their own needs, views and feelings, and be sensitive to the needs, views and feelings of others.*

Homes

Scuttling Spider (page 71)
The ideas in this poem would create a wonderful display showing the different homes on land and at sea, with the appropriate verse placed next to each home. Involve children in painting, drawing, cutting, gluing, and folding with a wide range of materials to produce a piece of work as a group.
CD – *To express and communicate their ideas, thoughts and feelings by using a widening range of materials, and suitable tools.*

In Granny's Garden (page 72)
Set up a place in the home corner and call it 'Granny's garden'. Place tall pot plants, or twigs in pots inside. Provide a birch broom, log, blanket and salt-dough 'food' and encourage children to play there.
CD – *To use their imagination in role play.*

My House (page 73)
Involve children in making up a poem based on the words 'My house ...'.
Write their ideas on a flip chart as they offer suggestions and then read it back to them.
CLL – *To make up their own rhymes and poems.*

Make the Bed (page 74)
Ask children to think about their own homes and everyday tasks. Together, write a list of things which make these tasks easier. For example, duvets instead of blankets; mops instead of scrubbing brushes; vacuum cleaners, dishwashers, washing machines, cookers, microwaves etc.
KUW – *To identify features in the place they live.*

Journeys

The Train Journey (page 75)

In a large space, ask children to hold each other around the waist in lines of three. Spread the lines of children around to represent different trains. Read the poem slowly at first, build up speed, and then slow down again and stop. Encourage children to control both their speed to fit the rhyme, and their direction so that they do not bump into each other.

PD – *To move with control and co-ordination.*

Farm Journey (page 76)

Draw two parallel lines across a large sheet of sugar paper and place up to ten small world cows on one row (i.e. following the leader). Place a smaller number of small toy vehicles or other animals on the other row. Encourage children to count up, and compare the number of items in each row using the words 'more' and 'less'.

MD – *To use language such as 'more' or 'less' to compare two numbers or quantities.*

Travelling (page 77)

Focus on the action words in the poem, such as 'racing', 'rolling', 'creeping', 'crawling' and in a large space invite children to try them out. Discuss less familiar words such as 'roaring', 'thundering' and 'snaking'. Can children suggest animals these words might be used with – such as lions, elephants, snakes and therefore what the vehicles and animals have in common?

CLL – *To explore the meaning and sounds of new words.*

Magic Carpet (page 78)

Sit with children on a brightly coloured carpet or cloth, and ask them to 'pretend' to see and taste the lovely places in the poem. Ask them to suggest other places to visit. Invite them to design a pattern for a carpet using crayons on sugar paper and show it to the group. Place a small toy on top and discuss an imaginary journey.

CD – *To use imagination in art, design and role play.*

There Goes the Train (page 79)

Discuss the train journey in the poem. Display different forms of transport using pictures and small toys. Each day consider the advantages and disadvantages of using one form of transport, inviting children to contribute from their experiences. Finally, ask children to record their favourite journey in a drawing.

KUW – *To look at similarities and differences.*

People

The Doctor (page 80)
Set up a toy's hospital and encourage children to role play doctors, nurses, ambulance staff and receptionists. Discuss how people feel when they are unwell, and what helps them to feel better.
PSED – *To have a developing awareness of their own needs, views and feelings, and be sensitive to the needs, views and feelings of others.*

Farmer, Farmer (page 81)
Discuss the busy day of the farmer and the importance of rest. Encourage children to describe active days of their own, and their need for food, rest and sleep to promote health and energy.
PD – *To recognize those things which contribute to keeping healthy.*

Who Am I? (page 82)
Chalk out streets and pedestrian crossings in an open space and invite children to role play drivers, pedestrians and crossing patrol people. Provide trikes, scooters and trucks etc and encourage observation of space and courtesy.
PD – *To show awareness of space, of themselves and others.*

The Chip Shop Man (page 83)
Write 'chip' and 'shop' at the top of a flip chart. Say the words, emphasizing the initial sound of each. Invite children to repeat ch, ch, ch, and then think of other words which begin with the same sound. Write their suggestions under the word 'chip'. Repeat with 'shop'. Remind children of these words and their initial sounds regularly, and add new words as they occur.
CLL – *To hear and say initial sounds.*

Seasons

Patterns on the Sand (page 84)
This poem links winter to summer through memories. It suggests ways of recalling occasions through the senses of sight, hearing and touch. Create a collection of shells and pebbles. Discuss their shapes and colours, and 'listen' to the songs/sounds heard from shells placed to the ear. Provide opportunities for children to express their responses through music and painting patterns and shapes.
CD – *To use imagination in art, design and music.*

The Scarecrow (page 85)
Show a picture of a scarecrow and talk about how and why he scares away crows. Discuss what would happen to seeds without him. Invite suggestions about what else birds could eat. Set up an experiment outside the window, planting grass seed in a large pot. Make a small scarecrow and place it in the pot. Nearby, place a bird table with seeds and nuts. Observe and compare the actions of the birds each day.
KUW – *To ask questions about why things happen.*

Autumn's Here! (page 86)

Use real conkers, fir cones and acorns for counting activities. Involve children in creating a large paper tree for display. Make coloured leaves and place some on the branches and some at the base. Count and compare each group. Cut and colour a squirrel and nuts for the display. Change the quantities, and count the number of leaves and nuts each day.

MD – *To count reliably up to 10 and use the language 'more' or 'less' to compare two numbers.*

New Life (page 87)

Create a farm using small world animals, pens and fences on green sugar paper; include improvised ponds, nests, trees, etc. Involve children in setting up the animals using the language in the poem. Discuss words such as 'meadow', 'paddock', 'orchard', 'blossom' and 'catkins', and animal names such as piglets and foals, which may not be familiar to children.

CLL – *To extend vocabulary and explore the meaning of new words.*

Jack Frost (page 88)

Show monochrome pictures of wintry, frosty days and spider's webs. Let children handle pieces of white lace and compare to the web pictures. Discuss the way the natural landscape is often black and white in winter. Provide black sugar paper and white paint and encourage children to express their ideas about the poem and the pictures.

CD – *To express and communicate ideas through painting.*

Shapes

Look at Shapes (page 89)

Ask children to draw round their own fingers (hands) and toes (feet), and round templates of an arm, leg, elephant, tree and mouse on a variety of coloured sugar paper, and cut them out. Draw round a child and cut that out too. Involve children in arranging an imaginative display of all these shapes, handling and discussing them as they do so.

CD – *To explore colour, shape, form and space in two dimensions.*

Shape that Dough (page 90)

Help children to use playdough or Plasticine in ways suggested in the poem.

PD – *To handle malleable materials with increasing control.*

Night and Day Shapes (page 91)

Cut out silver shapes of stars and moons in different stages of the month, and let children handle them. Explain that stars are really round but look star-shaped from a distance, and how the moon changes shape. On a sunny day investigate and identify a variety of shadows.

KUW – *To observe, find out about and identify features in the natural world.*

Drawing Shapes (page 92)

Involve children in seeking out and collecting circles such as saucers and lids and create a display of them in different sizes. Use plastic circles, squares and triangles for handling and pattern-making. Encourage children to experiment with rolling circles. Look for these shapes in the environment.

MD – *To use language such as 'circle', 'triangle', 'square' to describe shape.*

Songs and Games

Sailing on the Ocean (page 93)

In a large space, divide children into groups of waves, boats, sailors, flags and fish. Sit on mats. Sing the song together and, as each group's name is mentioned, that group perform their action on or around their mat. For example, the waves move in and out of their mat. On the words 'Sailing on the ocean', all groups run round their mat.

PD – *To move with confidence and safety.*

Twinkle, Twinkle, Christmas Lights (page 94)

Remind children of the original rhyme, 'Twinkle, Twinkle, Little Star' and ask them to think how this rhyme is different. Invite children to suggest other songs and rhymes they know. Do they know any different words for rhymes such as 'Humpty Dumpty'? Make up some nonsense rhymes together based on original rhymes or songs.

CLL – *To listen with enjoyment to songs and rhymes and make up some of their own.*

Here's a Toy Box! (page 95)

Involve children in covering a large cardboard box and decorating it. Create a lid and place different toys inside. Sing the song together, adapting the words to fit a toy removed from the box by one of the children. Encourage the group to tell a story about that toy.

CD – *To use their imagination in art, design and stories.*

The Horse Post (page 96)

Talk about the way post used to be delivered on horseback, and how it is delivered today. Invite in a postman to show his uniform and bag, and discuss the way post is collected and sorted. Invite children to bring in used envelopes to investigate postmarks and stamps.

KUW – *To find out about past and present events.*

Spider, Spider (page 97)

Use books or look at the shape and patterns of spider's webs outside. Discuss how hardworking and persistent the spider has to be to weave its web. Explain the harmlessness of spiders, and their use in eating flies. Encourage children to say whether it is right or wrong to destroy webs or other natural homes.

PSED – *To understand what is right, what is wrong, and why.*

Dawdling Dinosaurs (page 98)

Read the poem, emphasizing the initial letter sound 'd'. Write the letter on a flip chart. Read again slowly, asking children to say which words in the poem begin with this sound. List them on the chart. Ask them to suggest other animal words beginning with 'd', e.g. 'dog', 'duck', 'donkey', 'dolphin'. Say the poem together substituting different animals. Add descriptive words beginning with 'd', such as 'dancing', 'dotty', 'drooping'. Mix and substitute words in the poem, e.g. 'Dotty donkey danced'.
CLL – *To hear and say initial sounds in words.*

Special Things

My Bear (page 99)

Hold a 'Share Bear' day when children bring in a teddy they are willing to share for one day. Ask children to show their bear, and say why it is special. Explain the importance of caring for other people's bears, then allow children to choose a bear. After an hour, call in the bears and choose again. Return to owner at end of day.
PSED – *To work as part of a group taking turns and sharing fairly.*

These Are My Special Things (page 100)

Discuss the special things mentioned in the poem, and invite each child to choose the one they like best. Ask them to draw a picture and make up a story about it to tell to the others. Repeat with other things which are special to them not in the poem.
CD – *To use imagination in art and stories.*

My Tiny Treasures (page 101)

Collect or make all the items mentioned in the poem and place inside a cloth bag. Invite different children to take out specified numbers of items up to 10, counting them out as they do so. Reverse, by counting them back in small quantities. Ask children to bring in ten special tiny treasures of their own in a bag or shoe box, and use for similar counting and adding-on activities.
MD – *To count reliably up to ten objects.*

My Grandma (page 102)

Invite children to draw a picture of a person, place or event which is special to them, and talk to the group about why it is special, and what they like about it.
PSED – *To express needs and feelings.*

Weather

Rainbow, Rainbow (page 103)

On a sunny day, create a mini-rainbow outside using a garden hose. Explain how colours are seen when sun shines through water. Show children a peacock's feather, and discuss the colours of butterflies. Ask children to paint a large rainbow, using as many colours as they choose.
KUW – *To investigate objects using all their senses appropriately.*

Winter Weather (page 104)
Choose an appropriate winter's day to match each verse of the poem. Look outside and discuss what can be seen. Invite children to suggest and find suitable colours and materials for them to represent the weather in collage.
PSED – *To select and use activities and resources independently.*

The Wind Wizard (page 105)
Talk about the movement words of 'whooshing', 'weaving', 'whirling', 'waltzing' etc in the poem, and in a large space encourage children to think of ways to imitate these movements. Where appropriate, provide equipment to facilitate actions, such as obstacles to weave around.
PD – *To move with control and co-ordination.*

A Puddle Full of Raindrops (page 106)
The poem uses unusual ways of measuring capacity. Discuss together other fun ways of measuring full or empty. For example, a glove full of fingers, a jumper full/empty of child, a sleeve full/empty of arm, a boot full of leg.
MD – *To use appropriate language to compare capacity.*

Puddles (page 107)
Use one large wall to create a display of 'puddles' by the children. Draw around a variety of coloured papers to represent shiny, muddy, icy etc in a range of different sizes. Help children to use scissors to cut around the puddles, giving larger shapes to the less skilled. Provide left-and right-handed scissors and allow children to choose which sort they use.
PD – *To persevere in repeating actions to develop a new skill and show a clear preference for left or right hand.*

Early Learning Goals Summary Chart

PSED – Personal, Social and Emotional Development
CLL – Communication, Language and Literacy
MD – Mathematical Development
KUW – Knowledge and Understanding of the World
PD – Physical Development
CD – Creative Development

Theme and Rhymes	Page	PSED	CLL	MD	KUW	PD	CD
All About Me							
I Can Do Opposites	26		●				
My Hands, My Feet	27					●	
Show Five Fingers	28			●			
Gloves	29	●					
I Can Make Noises	30	●					
Animals and Mini-beasts							
Just a Taste?	31	●					
Rapping in the Jungle	32						●
Finger Farm	33		●				
Spider, Spider, Spinning Well	34				●		
Jungle Wood	35			●			
Mini-beasts	36				●		
Changes							
Caterpillar, Caterpillar	37						●
All Is Quiet	38		●				
Clouds	39				●		
Changing Sands	40					●	
When I Was Born	41					●	
Colours							
Let's Climb up a Rainbow	42						●
The Mehndi Tree	43						●
Painting Pictures	44			●			
Colours Here and Colours There	45		●				
Counting Rhymes							
Finger Teddies	46			●			
Down in the Jungle	47			●			
One Little Monkey	48			●			
Countdown to Bedtime	49	●					

Theme and Rhymes	Page	PSED	CLL	MD	KUW	PD	CD
Day and Night							
About Time!	50		●				
Stepping Through the Day	51				●		
When the Sun Steals Away	52					●	
When Night Comes	53				●		
Day and Night	54						●
Family							
Family Barbecue	55	●					
Over the Sea	56					●	
Family Lunch	57			●			
I Have a Baby Sister	58				●		
Am I the Tallest?	59			●			
Festivals							
Eid Mubarak (Happy Eid)	60	●					
Candles for Hanukkah	61						●
I've Made a Star	62		●				
The Dragon Dance	63		●				
Apple Bobbing	64				●		
Food and Shopping							
The Market	65		●				
I'm the Butcher	66				●		
I Love Bread	67			●			
Chocolate	68	●					
A Fruit to Suit?	69					●	
Dear Potato	70	●					
Homes							
Scuttling Spider	71						●
In Granny's Garden	72						●
My House	73		●				
Make the Bed	74				●		
Journeys							
The Train Journey	75					●	
Farm Journey	76			●			
Travelling	77		●				
Magic Carpet	78						●
There Goes the Train	79				●		

Theme and Rhymes	Page	PSED	CLL	MD	KUW	PD	CD
People							
The Doctor	80	●					
Farmer, Farmer	81					●	
Who Am I?	82					●	
The Chip Shop Man	83		●				
Seasons							
Patterns on the Sand	84						●
The Scarecrow	85				●		
Autumn's Here!	86			●			
New Life	87		●				
Jack Frost	88						●
Shapes							
Look at Shapes	89						●
Shape that Dough	90					●	
Night and Day Shapes	91				●		
Drawing Shapes	92			●			
Songs and Games							
Sailing on the Ocean	93					●	
Twinkle, Twinkle, Christmas Lights	94		●				
Here's a Toy Box!	95						●
The Horse Post	96				●		
Spider, Spider	97	●					
Dawdling Dinosaurs	98		●				
Special Things							
My Bear	99	●					
These Are My Special Things	100						●
My Tiny Treasures	101			●			
My Grandma	102	●					
Weather							
Rainbow, Rainbow	103				●		
Winter Weather	104	●					
The Wind Wizard	105					●	
A Puddle Full of Raindrops	106			●			
Puddles	107					●	

I Can Do Opposites

I can stand up   *Stand up straight.*

Or I can sit down   *Sit.*

I can smile   *Smile.*

Or I can frown   *Frown.*

I can run   *Run on the spot.*

Or I can walk   *Walk on the spot.*

I can be quiet   *Place finger on lips.*

Or I can talk   *Use fingers to 'chatter'.*

I can be happy   *Smile and sway happily.*

Or I can be sad   *Look very sad or pretend to cry.*

I can taste good things   *Pretend to eat something delicious.*

Or I can taste bad   *Screw up face as if tasting something bitter.*

I can jump in   *Jump forwards.*

Or I can jump out   *Jump back.*

I can *whisper*   *Cup hand to mouth as though whispering.*

Or I can **shout!**   *Shout last word.*

My Hands

My hands can stroke a teddy
My hands can hold a brush
My hands can help another
My hands are soft to touch.

My Feet

My feet can run, my feet can ride.
My feet can climb, my feet can slide.
My feet can dance, my feet can hop.
My feet can walk, my feet can stop.

Show Five Fingers

Show five fingers
> Let me see

Hold up one hand.

Look at children, who hold hand higher.

Show four fingers
> Touch your knee

Hold up four fingers.

Use these four fingers to touch knee.

Show three fingers
> Touch your nose

Hold up three fingers.

Use these three fingers to touch nose.

Show two fingers
> Touch your toes

Hold up two fingers.

Use these two fingers to touch toes.

Show one finger
> Let me see

Hold up one finger.

Look at children, who hold finger higher.

With this finger
> Point to me!

Waggle hand with finger extended.

Adult points to self, children point to adult.

Gloves

My gloves are in a muddle

And I'm trying to sort them out.

I turned them to the other side

But now they're inside out!

I tried to turn them back again

But now it seems to me

That where there were five fingers

There now are only three!

Demonstrate to children with a pair of gloves. Have one glove showing all five fingers but tuck two fingers on the other glove inside.

Children to show first five fingers and then three.

I Can Make Noises

Mime sounds.

I can laugh
I can cry

I can sing
I can sigh

I can cough
I can sneeze

I can even
Knock my knees!   *Knock knees together.*

I can shout
I can clap   *Clap quietly.*

I can make
My feet tap tap   *Tap feet on floor.*

I can whistle
I can speak

I can hum
I can shriek

I can scream
and I can giggle

But most of all
I like to wriggle!   *Wriggle about noisily, shuffling feet.*

Just a Taste?

Let me *sniff*   *Touch nose and wriggle it.*
Said the rabbit
   With an apple that he'd found.

Let me *touch*   *Point with finger as though touching.*
Said the monkey
      As he slid down to the ground.

Let me *see*   *Circle eyes with fingers and look down.*
Said the bird
      Who was high up in the sky.

Let me *listen*   *Cup ears.*
Said the owl
      Who was very quiet and shy.

Let me *taste*   *Lick lips.*
Said the wolf
      Just a taste, very small...   *Show smallness by putting finger and*
                                              thumb together.

So they *sniffed*   *Wriggle nose.*

      And they *touched*   *Point finger.*

            And they *looked*   *Circle eyes.*

                  And they *listened...*   *Cup ears.*

But the wolf *tasted* nothing   *Head back, drop apple in.*
He just *swallowed* it all!   *Rub stomach gleefully.*

Rapping in the Jungle

Place children into five groups, representing monkeys, snakes, lizards, tigers and toucans.

Rapping in the jungle *All groups beat time with soft drumming of the fingers.*

Rapping to a beat

Rapping to the bongo drums

Rapping with your feet. *Beat time with feet.*

Rapping with the monkeys *Monkeys lift one arm as though hanging from a tree.*

Rapping with the snakes *Snakes slither on the floor.*

Rapping with the lizards *Lizards dart quickly forward on hands and knees.*

Rap for rapping's sake.

Rapping with the tigers *Tigers raise hands like claws and show teeth.*

And the toucan bird *Toucans make hands into a beak and open and shut.*

Rapping with the bongo drums *All groups beat with fingers.*

Make your rapping heard! *Beat loudly and shout out.*

Finger Farm

A finger rhyme

Here is the farmer leading the bull   *Point to each finger in turn.*

Here is the sheep to give us some wool

Here is the goose that waddles about

Here is the pig with a long pink snout

Here is the chicken pecking the corn

Here is the foal that has just been born

Here is the duck that swims in the pool

Here is the farm dog playing the fool

Here is the cow to give us some milk

Here is the cat with a coat of silk

Here is the farm   *Spread open hands side by side, palms upwards.*

and here is the house   *Place hands together prayer-like pointing upwards.*

and here at the door

is Thumb-thumb the mouse!   *Keep hands together and wiggle one thumb.*

Spider, Spider, Spinning Well

Spider, spider,
spinning well

Spread fingers like a spider.

Make circles in the air with forefinger.

Missed a stitch
and
down
she
fell

Spin finger downwards.

Falling,
falling
from the ceiling

Continue to spiral downwards.

Gave her such
a funny feeling!

Hold tummy.

Dingly,
dangling
from a thread

Hand upside down, fingers grasping imaginary thread,

swing hand from side to side.

Climbing,
climbing
to her web.

Climb back up the thread with fingers spider-shaped.

Jungle Wood

There are wild beasts
in Jungle Wood.
In the undergrowth.
They come in different sizes,
the bad ones and the good.

Stand in a circle.

Form hands into claw shapes. Look fierce.

Indicate 'small' and 'large' with fingers.
Look fierce, then smile kindly.

There's a spider, spinning spider's webs
with its secret spider spinner.
He hopes to catch a foolish fly
and eat him for his dinner!

Use hands to draw circles in the air,
moving outwards.
Make web with finger and thumb of one
hand. Trap a finger from other hand.

There's a snail making silver trails
with a snail's sneaky skimmer.
And, climbing on a flower stem,
a creeping caterpillar.

Trail a finger up one arm.

Creep one hand up the other arm.

There are hard-working armies,
of ants in long parades.
Trekking through the pathways
on food-hunting raids.

Turn, to form a trail of children.

Trek round in a circle.

There are wild beasts
in Jungle Wood.
But do not be afraid.
For these are tiny mini-beasts
Living in the shade.

Make hands into claw shapes. Look fierce.

Shake head.

Indicate smallness with finger and thumb.

Mini-beasts

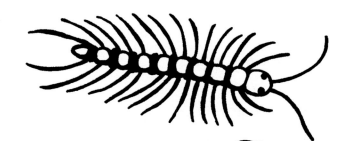
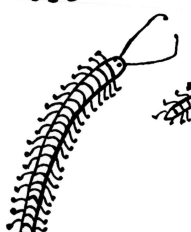

In a wood
that I know
there's a place
where bluebells grow.
Near the bluebells
there's a stone.
Underneath
there is a home.
Tiny woodlice,
centipedes,
earwigs, beetles,
millipedes.
Please be careful
if you're peeping.
Little creatures there
are sleeping.

Caterpillar, Caterpillar

Caterpillar, caterpillar

Crawling up a tree.

Make crawling actions upwards.

Caterpillar, caterpillar

Crawl on me.

Crawl fingers of hand up other arm.

Caterpillar, caterpillar

Curl up tight.

Curl into a ball.

Caterpillar, caterpillar

Sleep all night.

Pretend to sleep.

Caterpillar, caterpillar

When you wake

Wake and stretch.

Give your wings

A gentle shake.

Shake arms like wings.

Caterpillar, caterpillar

Don't be shy.

Shake head. Look shy.

Now you are a BUTTERFLY

Move arms gently and pretend to fly.

Fun with Action Rhymes and Poems

All Is Quiet

All is quiet
There is no sound,
Till someone starts to wriggle,
And then a little shuffle
As others start to giggle.

Then a tiny whisper
Which grows into a chat.
Someone hums a little tune
And beats time on the mat.

Someone starts to tickle
To make another shout.
After that talk grows and grows
Until there is no doubt

That quiet little girls and boys
Are now creating
Such a

NOISE!

CLOUDS

TINY WHITE CLOUDS   *Drift around, turning slowly.*
HIGH IN THE SKY
FLOATING LIKE FEATHERS
DAWDLING BY.

LOOK AT THE CLOUDS   *Grow taller and bigger.*
SEE HOW THEY GROW   *Move about touching each*
                           other occasionally.
DANCING TOGETHER
DRIFTING LOW.   *Stoop and turn.*

NOW BLACK CLOUDS
ARE STARTING TO   *Join hands in a circle.*
GATHER
                           Walk slowly round in circle.
THIS IS THE START
OF VERY WET WEATHER!

SOON THE CLOUDS   *Raise joined hands high.*
COVER THE SKY   *Form a tent with hands in the centre.*
DOWN FALL THE   *Release and drop hands*
                           downwards.
RAINDROPS.
PLOP! IN MY EYE!   *Look up and wipe eye.*

Changing Sands

Ask children to sit cross-legged on the floor and imagine sand in front of them.

I smooth the sand   *Make smoothing movements with hands.*
And give a pat   *Pat the floor.*
Until its lying
Straight and flat.   *Smooth hands along floor.*

And then I dig   *Mime digging.*
To make a heap   *Make the shape of a heap, with both hands.*
Of sand that's thick
And really deep.   *Pretend to plunge hands into deep sand.*

I fill my bucket   *Mime shovelling sand into a bucket.*
For a while
Then tip it out   *Pretend to upturn it.*
Into a pile

And there's a castle   *Indicate shape of castle with hands.*
High and tall.
So all around   *Draw a circle round imaginary castle, on the floor.*
I build a wall.

I love to play   *Hold hands up and wriggle fingers.*
And use my hands
To change the shape   *Mime running fingers through sand on floor.*
Of golden sand.

When I Was Born

When I was born,

I was so small.

I couldn't talk,

or walk at all.

I learnt to sit

and then to stand.

I held on tight

to Mummy's hand.

But now I skip

and jump and run.

I sing and laugh

and have such fun.

I hold a cup,

and eat my toast.

I help wash up,

and fetch the post.

I hold a pencil,

kick a ball.

I'm growing up.....

.......I'm really tall!

Let's Climb up a Rainbow

When sun shines on raindrops
Every colour is there
Creating a rainbow
Of magical stairs

Let's walk up a rainbow
Just take my hand
We'll climb up the colours
To a beautiful land

The Mehndi Tree

An Indian story and tradition, for Hindu brides, and celebrations

Place children in pairs.

Take red and gold of the morning skies

Reach up, pretending to take leaves.

from the leaves of the mehndi tree.

Mime stirring into paste.

Make patterns from these special dyes

on the hands of you and me.

Point to partner and then self.

Take little hands, and decorate

Hold out hands to partner.

with mango, leaves, and curls,

Take turns to make patterns with finger on partner's hands.

A paisley pattern of your own

with mehndi shapes and swirls.

Hold partner's hand and turn slowly.

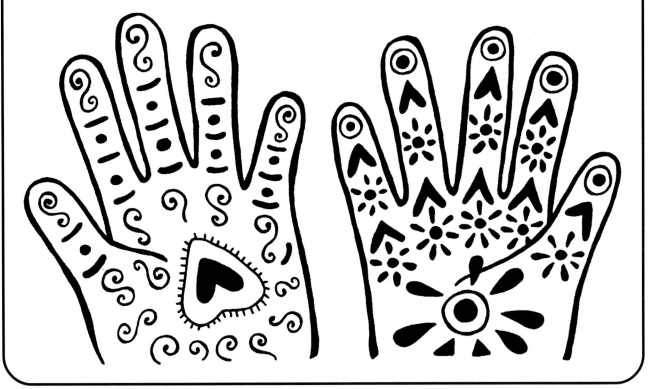

Fun with Action Rhymes and Poems

Painting Pictures

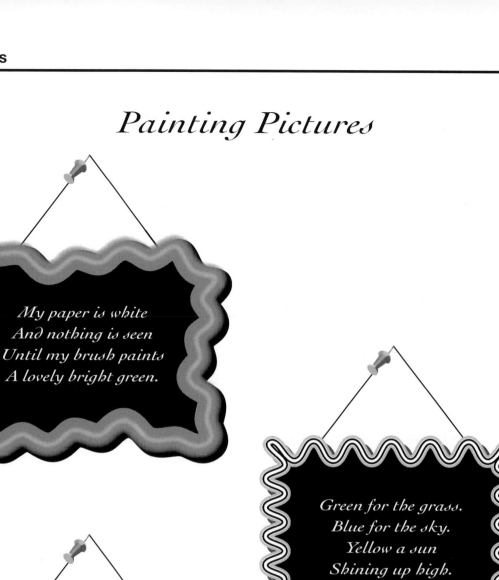

*My paper is white
And nothing is seen
Until my brush paints
A lovely bright green.*

*Green for the grass.
Blue for the sky.
Yellow a sun
Shining up high.*

*Red for a house.
Brown for a tree.
And there in the middle
A picture of me.*

*My paper now shows
A beautiful scene.
And to think it all started
By painting with green!*

Colours Here and Colours There

Colours here and colours there
Colours are just everywhere.

Purple hat, dark red tie
Yellow flowers, bright blue sky.

Orange sweater, scarlet socks
Stripy zebra, light brown fox.

After showers a rainbow bright
Multicoloured, shining light.

Speckled shadows on the lawn
Grey-green mountains, golden corn.

Silver cars and silver stars
Shiny fruits and jam in jars.

Red tomatoes, cabbage green
Jewellery with an amber sheen.

Patterned seas of many blues
Black and brown or pastel shoes.

Coloured candles on the cake
Light reflected on a lake.

Look around and you will see
Every colour there can be.

Finger Teddies

Here is teddy number one

Show thumb of one hand.

He can beat upon a drum.

Move thumb inwards to beat on palm of hand.

Here is teddy number two

Hold up first finger.

He is pointing straight at you.

Point at other children.

Here is teddy number three

Touch second finger with finger of the other hand .

He's the tallest one you see.

Hold hand out to see length of this finger compared to others.

Here is teddy number four

Clench third finger with other hand.

Hold this teddy in your paw.

Last of all is teddy five

Show smallest finger.

He can quickly curl and hide.

Curl up this finger and make a clenched fist.

DOWN IN THE JUNGLE

Place children in a circle with one child in the centre.

DOWN IN THE JUNGLE
CAN YOU HEAR THE RUMBLE?
HERE COME THE ELEPHANTS
ONE, TWO, THREE.

Children walk round in circle, with heavy steps, swinging one arm as a trunk.

All children count, as child in centre calls in three elephants.

DOWN IN THE JUNGLE
CAN YOU HEAR THEM GRUMBLE?
HERE COME THE ALLIGATORS
ONE, TWO, THREE.

Repeat above, but using arms to mimic jaws of alligator opening and closing.

All children count, as three alligators are called in.

DOWN IN THE JUNGLE
CAN YOU HEAR THEM MUMBLE?
HERE COME THE SPIDER MONKEYS
ONE, TWO, THREE.

Repeat again, moving arms to mimic monkeys swinging through trees.

All children count, as three monkeys are called in.

DOWN IN THE JUNGLE
HAVE A ROUGH AND TUMBLE,
ANIMALS ARE GATHERING
TO HAVE THEIR TEA.

Children who've been called into centre hold hands and dance around child in the middle.

DOWN IN THE JUNGLE
EATING APPLE CRUMBLE,
COUNT ALL THE ANIMALS
STANDING IN A LINE.

All children pretend to eat.

Animals line up. Child in centre points to each one in turn as all children count.

1, 2, 3, 4, 5, 6, 7, 8, NINE!

Fun with Action Rhymes and Poems

One Little Monkey

Children hold hands in a circle, and chant the rhyme as they walk round one child in the middle.

One little monkey
Cannot stop
Climbing up a tree
To the very top.

*Child in middle kneels down
and makes climbing movements
with arms and hands.*

Climbing higher
Climbing well
Came a clap of thunder
And down he fell.

*Child in the middle stands up
and continues climbing movement using legs
and arms, and reaching higher and higher.*

All other children clap hands loudly.

All fall down.

Two little monkeys *etc*

until ... And down they fell.

*Child in the middle chooses another child to
join him.*

Repeat, up to ten little monkeys.

Countdown to Bedtime

One to cuddle	*Cuddle arms around self.*
Two to touch	*Stroke own hair.*
Three, I love you very much.	*Lean forward to whisper 'I love you very much'.*
Four to kiss	*Blow a kiss..*
Five to hug	*Hug self.*
Six, to snuggle like a bug	*Lie down and snuggle up arms and legs.*
Seven to whisper	*Put hand to mouth as though whispering.*
Eight to creep	*Creep fingers along floor to mime parent leaving room.*
Nine to wish a goodnight's sleep!	*Put hands under head and pretend to sleep.*

About Time!

It's ...

put your toys away time   *Pretend to pick up toys and place on shelves,*

climbing up the stairs time   *climb on the spot,*

splashing in the bath time   *splash water over selves and others,*

brushing up your teeth time   *brush teeth,*

jumping into bed time   *jump once on the spot,*

read a story book time   *read a book,*

putting out the light time   *switch off the light,*

looking at the moon time   *draw a circle in the air,*

talking to yourself time   *waggle head and pretend to talk,*

wriggling in the bed time   *wriggle about.*

'Can I have a drink?' time   *Speak questioningly and mime drinking,*

Mummy's getting cross time   *put hands on hips and look cross,*

time to go to sleep time   *lie down,*

Goodnight!   *wave fingers and close eyes.*

Stepping Through the Day

Finger rhyme or action rhyme: count on fingers, or take one step forwards for each number.

ONE is for morning — the day has begun

TWO is for daylight and bright shiny sun

THREE is for breakfast and
buttery toast

FOUR is for letters that come in the post

FIVE is for friends who come round to play

SIX is for lunch we eat at mid-day

SEVEN is for books and pictures to see

EIGHT is for later with ice cream for tea

NINE is for bathtime and water that's deep

TEN is for bedtime and children asleep

Fun with Action Rhymes and Poems

When the Sun Steals Away

Children stand one in front of another in a circle.

When the sun steals away

Children creep round following each other in the circle.

At the end of the day

Turn inwards and stand still.

And her bright golden rays

Sweep both arms upwards and outwards then let them rest in front.

softly fade

Then the moon knows it's time

Use one arm to make a circle in front.

To begin her steep climb

Mime climbing, using arms and legs.

And the stars join her silver

Join hands in the circle and gently rock from side to side.

parade.

Fun with Action Rhymes and Poems

© Brenda Williams

When Night Comes

When night comes
Then lights are seen
Big round moon
And lighthouse beam

When night comes
A torch shines bright
Cat's eyes glisten
In reflected light

When night comes
Headlights flitter
Stars sparkle
Street lights glitter

When night comes
Candles glow
Gentle glimmer
Of lamps turned low

When night comes
Then lights awake
Shimmer and shine
Until daybreak

Fun with Action Rhymes and Poems

Day and Night

Here is the sun that shines by day

Form a circle with fingers and thumbs of both hands together.

Here are the children out at play

Clap hands and skip about.

Here are the birds that flap and fly

Move arms up and down.

Here is a fluttering butterfly

Link thumbs and flutter spread hands.

Here is the moon that shines at night

Form a circle with fingers and thumbs of both hands together.

Here are the children with eyes shut tight

Put two hands together beside head and close eyes.

Here are the birds asleep in their nest

Have feet together, hands folded in front, head down.

Here is the butterfly having a rest

Link thumbs, spread hands then gently close them together.

Family Barbecue

Invite children to stand in a circle.

Mummy	*Hold up:*
	one finger
Daddy	*two fingers*
Baby too,	*three fingers*
Grandma	*four fingers*
Grandpa	*five fingers*
Sister Sue,	*six fingers*
Auntie Anne	*seven fingers*
And Uncle Lou,	*eight fingers*
Jenny	*nine fingers*
Jack	*ten fingers.*
Quite a few,	*Wriggle fingers about in front.*
Coming to	*Hold hands and dance in a circle*
Our barbecue.	*for last two lines.*

Fun with Action Rhymes and Poems

Over the Sea

Over the sea
Over the sea
I'm going to see
My family.

Stand in a circle. Make wavy movements with arms.

Point to self.

In distant lands
So far away
That is where
My family stay.

Have hands above eyes, looking around.

Point to self.

But soon
Quite soon
Come sun or rain
We'll be a family
again.

Make the shape of a sun then flutter fingers downwards like rain.

Join hands together.

Over the sea
Over the sea
I'm going to see
My family.

Keep hands joined and dance around together.

Family Lunch

Invite children to role play the different family members.

Lay the table carefully,
How many are there
Let me see…
There's Daddy and Mummy –
That makes two,
Then there's me
And then there's you.
Now I've counted up to four
Who's that knocking on the door?
It's Uncle John and Auntie Trix –
How many now?
I think that's six.
Are there any more to come?
Grandma and Grandpa, you are late!
Two more places
That makes eight.
Cousin Jake and little Ben!
Come inside,
You make it ten.

Fun with Action Rhymes and Poems

I Have a Baby Sister

I have a baby sister

Who is very very new

Her face is pink and wrinkly

And I think her eyes are blue.

I peeped at little sister

As she lay in my old cot

She's really rather tiny

And doesn't say a lot.

I offered her my finger

She waved and held on tight

I have a brand new sister

Who only came last night.

Am I the Tallest?

My sister is taller than me

Place hand just above head.

My brother is taller than her

Place hand even higher, stretching up.

But am I taller than both of them...

Point to self, looking smug.

If I stand upon the chair?

Stand on small chair.

Eid Mubarak (Happy Eid)

*The festival of Eid-ul-Fitr comes at the end of Ramadan and marks the end of fasting.
The festival starts when the new moon appears – and crowds gather to watch for it.
Cards sent to mark this festival often carry the greeting Eid Mubarak (Happy Eid).*

Can you see the new moon   *Place hand above eyes and look upwards, searching.*

Shining in the night?

Can you see the new moon

Showing us its light?

Now the fast is over   *Place hand over mouth.*

And we shall have great fun   *Fling arms out wide.*

Sending everyone a card   *Pretend to give cards to each other.*

And meeting everyone.   *Smile or hug each other.*

We shall wear our best clothes   *Move hands over clothes, showing them off.*

And there'll be lots of sweets,   *Cup hands together.*

We will have a holiday   *Hold hands and dance around.*

And eat up lovely treats!   *Sit down and pretend to eat.*

Candles for Hanukkah

*The Jewish festival of Hanukkah takes place in December. It lasts for eight days.
The Menorah or candlestick has nine branches, but the centre one is used to light the others –
one candle on the first night, two candles on the second and so on.*

Nine special branches

On our candle tree

Eight are for Hanukkah

Please light one for me.

Please light two for me etc up to eight candles.

Fun with Action Rhymes and Poems

I've Made a Star

I've made a star
And pretty things
And bought a doll
With angel wings.

S i l v e r   t i n s e l
B a u b l e s   b r i g h t
S o m e   t i n k l i n g   b e l l s
A n d   c o l o u r e d   l i g h t s .

W e ' v e   w o o d e n   t o y s
A n d   t i n y   t r e a t s
C h r i s t m a s   c r a c k e r s
A n d   l i t t l e   s w e e t s .

So now we're off
To fetch our tree
Then Christmas time
Is here for me!

The Dragon Dance

Chinese New Year is the first and most important of the traditional Chinese festivals. It falls on the first day of the first lunar month of the year, which can be in January or February.

Fasten red and gold paper streamers to the wrists of children before starting.

Dragon, dragon
Darting dragon
Dancing through the town

Adult leads children in a dragon line, heads down towards back of child in front and holding their waist, and moving and dancing round in a circle.

Dragon, dragon
Dashing dragon
Dipping up and down

Stay in line, but dip knees and then rise upwards on tiptoe to give dipping movement.

Dragon, dragon
Bright and bold
Flame red eyes
Scales of gold

Stop the dragon in a big circle and face inwards. Look strong and fierce.
Point to eyes.
Stroke clothes.

Dragon whirling
Dragon swirling
Curling, twirling
Round and round

Move arms in big circles to make streamers fly.
Continue the movement and turn on the spot, leaning outwards and swirling streamers.

Dragon, dragon
Fiery dragon
You give me no fear

Hold hands and move around in a circle.

Dragon, dragon
Lucky dragon
Bringing in New Year!

Stand still and move arms forwards in wavy dragon movements.
Emphasize 'Lucky'.
Shout 'New Year' and fling arms outwards.

Apple Bobbing

Water in the barrel

Water up my nose

Water on my hair

Water on my clothes

Apples in the water

Bobbing underneath

Apples in the barrel

But not between my teeth!

The Market

Ribbons and hairbands
Buttons and lace
Biscuits and dog food
Each in their place.

Dustpans and brushes
Buckets and bowls
Bright patterned carpets
And long thin poles.

Cushions and curtains
Shoes and clothes
Dolls and tall teddies
Standing in rows.

Apples and melons
Flowers and meat
All in the market
Along the main street.

Fun with Action Rhymes and Poems

I'm the Butcher

I'm the butcher
Down your street,
Come to me
To buy your meat.

Chicken, beef,
Nice lamb chop,
Sausage, pies,
In my shop.

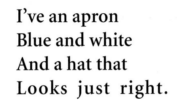

I've an apron
Blue and white
And a hat that
Looks just right.

I slice the bacon,
Stack the eggs
And place in trays
The turkey legs.

When you're passing
Do call in
To choose fresh meat
Or buy a tin.

I'm the butcher
Down your street,
Come to me
To buy your meat!

I Love Bread

A nonsense rhyme

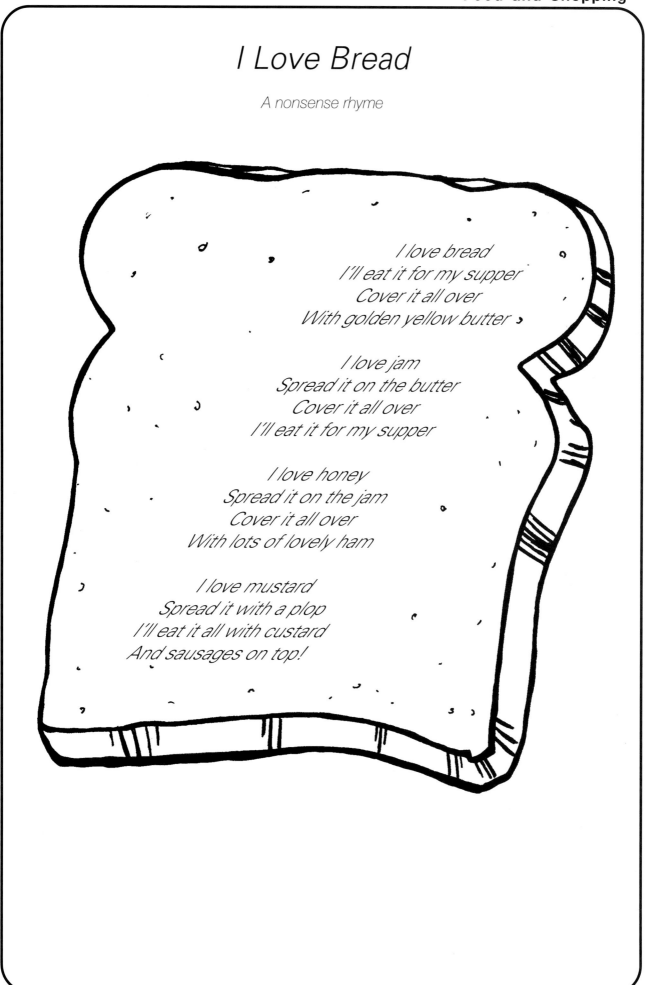

I love bread
I'll eat it for my supper
Cover it all over
With golden yellow butter

I love jam
Spread it on the butter
Cover it all over
I'll eat it for my supper

I love honey
Spread it on the jam
Cover it all over
With lots of lovely ham

I love mustard
Spread it with a plop
I'll eat it all with custard
And sausages on top!

Fun with Action Rhymes and Poems

Chocolate

Chocolate is yummy
Chocolate is good
I'd eat it all day
If only I could!

Chocolate for breakfast
Chocolate for tea
Chocolate for supper
Chocolate for me!

Chocolate is scrummy
Chocolate is great
But don't give me cabbage
That's something I hate!

A Fruit to Suit?

A banana is a fruit
In a yellow zip-off suit
While apples wear a coat
Of red or green.

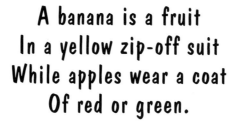

A strawberry wears a hat
Which is green and rather flat
But grapes are the friendliest
Fruit I've seen.

For they gather in a bunch
You can eat them for your lunch
And their over-coats have a red
Or yellow sheen.

An orange wears thick leather
In every kind of weather
While plums have a dress
Of velveteen.

Cherries do not come alone
Though they have a heart of stone
And their anoraks have a black
And shiny gleam.

But when fruit is on parade
It's the peach all cloaked in suede
That we love to eat for tea
With soft ice-cream!

Fun with Action Rhymes and Poems

Dear Potato

You're round and brown
And firm to touch
But oh, I like you
Very much!

I like you boiled
All soft and white.
I like you mashed
With butter bright.

I like you baked
With crusty skin
Or cut and sliced up
Very thin
And sold as crisps
In shops.
My dear potato,
You're the tops!

But I must tell you
What is best,
What tastes much better
Than the rest.

The taste I love
Upon my lips
Is when you're chopped
And fried as chips!

Scuttling Spider

Scuttling spider, light and small
Weaves his web against the wall.

Bright—eyed bird, flying free
Makes his nest high in a tree.

Long—eared rabbit, soft and round
Builds a burrow underground.

Shiny, slippy, slimy snail
Has a shell for head and tail.

Leaping frog, green and cool
Likes to live beside a pool.

Spouting whale with swishing motion
Lives his life within an ocean.

Blindly tunnelling tiny mole
Sleeps below ground in a hole.

All have homes where they can rest
But I think that my house is best!

Fun with Action Rhymes and Poems

In Granny's Garden

In Granny's garden is a place
Where I have found a special space.

Under the leaves of a bent old tree
I've made a house for you and me.

We'll sweep the floor with our twig broom,
We'll dust and tidy every room.

The branches we can use as shade
While you and I drink lemonade.

A little log can be our seat,
We'll make pretend food we can't eat.

We'll live forever in our tree
Till Granny calls us in for tea!

MY HOUSE

MY HOUSE IS SO TALL *Stand on tiptoe reaching up.*

MY HOUSE HAS A WALL *Spread arms and legs wide.*

MY HOUSE HAS A DOOR *Pretend to open a door and walk through.*

MY HOUSE HAS A FLOOR *Stamp on ground.*

MY HOUSE HAS A TREE *Wave arms above head.*

MY HOUSE HAS ME! *Point to self.*

Make the Bed

Ask children to stand on one side of a large space or carpeted area.

Make the bed　　　　　　　　*Mime shaking duvet.*
Make the bed
Make the bed today

Make the bed
Make the bed
Then we go and play!　　　　*Run to the other side of area.*

Clean the floor　　　　　　*Kneel and make scrubbing movement.*
Clean the floor
Clean the floor today

Clean the floor
Clean the floor
Then we go and play!　　　*Run back to first side of area.*

Repeat with other activities and appropriate actions, for example:

Dust the shelves
Wash the cups
Iron the clothes
Cook the food

The Train Journey

The train is running on the

                track track track

And I'm sitting in the carriage at the

                back back back

For we're going on a journey that is

                fast fast fast

The fields and the cows whizz

                past past past

We're going to the seaside very

                quick quick quick

And I'm listening to the wheels as they

                click click click

And we're going over hills to the

                top top top

But slowly......

       very slowly......

         we come to a station and we

                  stop...

                      stop...

                        stop!

Read quickly to a beat. Children stamp or clap to the last three words in each line, but slow down and quieten to a whisper as they stop.

Farm Journey

Ask two children to stand facing each other with arms forming a bridge to represent the barn door (last verse). Depending on numbers, other pairs of children could form a gate, a hedge, a yard. Say the poem together as you choose the cows that are named, and place the children in line (un-named children can fit in between the others). Then say the poem again as you lead them in a file, round the room and through the various openings. After passing through the barn doors, children are asked to sit down.

Follow the leader,
Follow the leader,
We are the cows
Going back to the farm.

Here is Molly,
Followed by Dolly,
Leading the others
Back to the farm.

Down the field,
Through the gate,
Time for milking,
Don't be late!

Here is Milly,
And here is Jilly,
Following others
Back to the farm.

Through the hedge
And down the lane,
Back to the farmer's
Yard again.

Here is Maisy,
And here is Daisy,
Feeling lazy
Last in line.

Follow the leader,
Follow the leader,
Through the yard
And into the barn!

Travelling

Roaring,
racing,
on the motorway,
Motorbike,
sports car,
speeding on their way.
Rolling,
bowling,
lorry with a load,
Oil tanker,
motorcoach,
thundering down the road.
Taxi-cab,
motor home,
pushing into place.
Braking,
snaking,
rushing in a race.

Creeping,
crawling,
through a country lane,
Tractor,
bicycle,
slowly, in the rain.
Cattle truck,
milk float,
broken-down old jeep,
Rambling,
scrambling,
a farmer's flock of sheep!

Fun with Action Rhymes and Poems

Magic Carpet

Sit on the carpet
And close your eyes
For this carpet is magic
And soon we will rise

We'll float far away
Where no-one has been
To see rivers of honey
And fields of ice-cream

Sugar-topped mountains
Blackcurrant seas
Banana-milk lakes
And chocolate trees

Whipped cream clouds
And lemonade rain
Then we open our eyes
And are back home again.

There Goes the Train

Invite children to sit or stand in a circle, with one or two others miming a train going from inside the circle and round the outside, before returning to the centre of the circle at the end.

There goes the train
Clickety clack
Out of the town
Along the track

Encourage children to clap to a beat.

Under bridges
Or motorway
Travelling fast
It's on its way

Form a bridge with arms, fingers just touching. Then fling arms outwards, horizontal and flat.

Through the fields
And countryside
Over the rivers
Wet and wide

Place hands together, prayer-like, moving them forwards and then apart and outwards.
Make a curving movement upwards and over, with one arm.

Into a tunnel
Under the hill
Out in the sunshine
Travelling still

Make a tunnel shape with one arm and push the other arm through it.

Here comes the train
Clickety clack
Back to the town
Along the track.

Repeat clapping to a beat.

The Doctor

Mime as suggested or role play.

Harry can't come out to play today *Shake head.*

Harry is feeling unwell *Look miserable.*

Harry has spots on his tummy *Point to tummy.*

Some on his bottom as well! *Point to bottom.*

Harry can't come out to play today *Shake head.*

Harry is staying in bed *Raise hands to side of face as though sleeping.*

Mummy has sent for the doctor *Pretend to phone.*

And here's what the doctor said:

Harry must take some medicine *Mime pouring medicine into spoon and swallowing.*

Harry will soon feel okay *Smile.*

Harry can play out tomorrow

But Harry can't play out today. *Shake head.*

For role play, choose:
a child to play Harry (substitute name as appropriate), child or children calling for Harry to play, mother answering door and phoning doctor, and a doctor. All children to join in the actions.

Farmer, Farmer

Farmer, farmer
Harvest the crops
Put into store
Or fill the shops.

Farmer, farmer
Up at dawn
Out in the fields
Cutting the corn.

Farmer, farmer
Works all day
Digging up carrots
And baling hay.

Farmer, farmer
Fruit to sell
Apples and pears
And plums as well.

Farmer, farmer
Out at night
Driving a tractor
In fading light.

Farmer, farmer
Go to bed!
Time to rest
Your weary head.

Who Am I?

I am a special person
A person that you know
I'm always there to meet you
In rain or sun or snow
I stand on zebra crossings
And make the traffic stop
I wear a special shiny coat
And wave a lollipop!

The Chip Shop Man

Chip, chop, chip
the chips

Drop them in fat
and lick your lips

Cover the fish
with flour and batter

Splash them in oil
with such a splatter

Watch them cook
to a golden glow

Sieve them out
and put on show

Salt and vinegar
Wrap them well

Such a warm
and tasty smell

The chip shop man
Makes chips just right

And we buy some
Every Friday night!

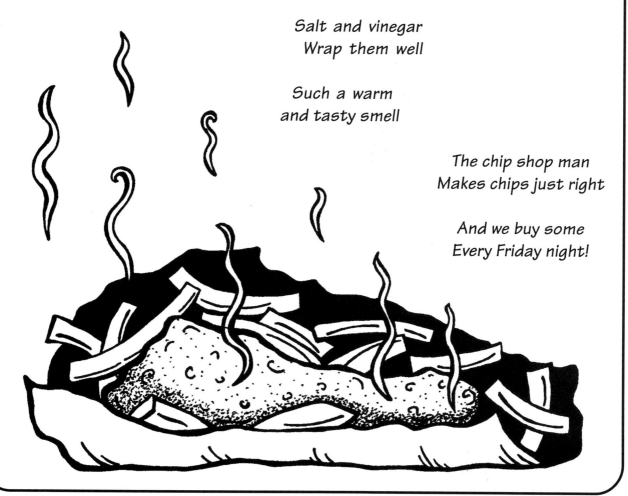

Fun with Action Rhymes and Poems

Patterns on the Sand

The
  sea
    made
      a pattern
        on the sand
          of ridges, swirls and waves.
        And I held tight
      to Mummy's hand
    as we wandered near to caves.
  And all along the shoreline
a pebbled pattern lay,
  shiny, white and curving,
    in the same shape as the bay.
      I found a shell in pink and pearl
        and traced my finger
          round its swirl.
      Now in winter
    after tea,
  the shell sings songs
about the sea.
I turn its colours
  in my hand,
    and think
      about that
        patterned
          sand.

The Scarecrow

I am a happy scarecrow
I stand here all the day
The only thing I have to do
Is scare the crows away.

My coat is all in tatters
My hat flaps to and fro
But the only thing that matters is
I scare away each crow.

I am a simple scarecrow
But you should really know
I have a most important job
I help the crops to grow.

The farmer made me out of sticks
And clothes he did not need
He planted me to guard his fields
And keep birds from his seeds.

I am a scary scarecrow
For that is what I do
I scare the crows and other birds
But..........

I hope I don't scare you!

Fun with Action Rhymes and Poems

Autumn's Here!

Wind and rain soak the grass,
Making puddles where I splash.

Coloured leaves of orange-red,
Make a hedgehog's cosy bed.

Hunting through the leafy ground,
There are fir cones to be found.

Shiny conkers, acorns too,
There's a treasure here for you!

See the squirrel, just like me,
Seeking nuts beneath the tree.

Autumn's here! The summer's gone.
Soon we'll see a wintry sun.

New Life

The lambs are in the meadow
The piglets in the pen
The foals are in the paddock
The chickens with the hen

There are ducklings on the water
And tadpoles growing legs
In every nest a mother bird
Is sitting on her eggs

There is blossom in the orchard
And catkins growing too
There are flowers in the garden
And all the world seems new

Fun with Action Rhymes and Poems

Jack Frost

He's been again   In the night   Painting windows   Sparkling white

Silver trees   And frosty paths   Crystal footprints   Spiky grass

Spider's webs   Of wintry lace   Jack Frost's touch   In every place

LO**O**k at Shapes

Look at the shape of my fingers	*Wiggle fingers about.*
Look at the shape of my nose	*Point to nose.*
Look at the shape of my arms and legs	*Shake arms and legs.*
Look at the shape of my toes	*Point to toes.*
Look at the shape of an elephant	*Wave arm around like a trunk.*
Look at the shape of a tree	*Spread arms like a tree.*
Look at the shape of a tiny mouse	*Curl up small.*
Then look at the shape of me!	*Jump up spreading arms and legs outwards.*

Fun with Action Rhymes and Poems

Shape that Dough

Roll, roll the playdough
See what you can make

Pretend to roll dough in both hands.

First a curly caterpillar
Then a long thin snake

Make wavy movements with hand.
Hold finger towards thumb to indicate thinness then move hand across in straight line.

Curve it in a circle
Add some eyes and nose

Draw big circle in the air.
Pretend to make it into a face by adding eyes and nose.

Squeeze it, squash it, shape it
That's the way it goes

Pretend to squeeze, squash and shape dough.

Roll it in your fingers
To shape a funny mouse

Pretend to roll dough in fingers.
Curl up like a mouse.

A square and a triangle
Will make a little house

Draw a square in the air, then a triangle above.

Roll out the playdough
See what you can make

Pretend to roll dough in your hands.

Roll it in a little ball
Then flatten it for a cake.

Pretend to make a ball, pass from one hand to the other.
Hold out one hand then clap down the other hand to flatten cake.

Night and Day Shapes

I like the shapes at night

The star shapes shining bright

I like the moon in all its shapes

For it gives a lovely light.

I like the shapes by day

When the round sun shines on me

I like the shapes of shadows

From house, and plants and tree.

Fun with Action Rhymes and Poems

Drawing Shapes

Draw a circle

Round and round

Roll the circle

On the ground.

Draw shape of circle in the air.

Keep drawing round and round.

Pretend to put the circle on the ground and roll it.

Draw a square

In the air

Draw four legs

And it's a chair.

Draw a square in the air.

Pretend to add four legs.

Pretend to take it out of the air and sit on it.

Draw a triangle
With three sides
Like a roof
Where you can hide.

Draw a triangle in the air.

Place hands above head to form an apex.

Stoop slightly with hands still forming roof.

Sailing on the Ocean

Sing to the tune of 'The wheels on the Bus'.

Children form a circle holding hands.

The waves on the sea
Splash in and out,
In and out,
In and out.
The waves on the sea
Splash in and out,
Sailing on the ocean.

Move in and out of circle, lifting hands upwards in the centre, and down at the edge
Repeat twice, quickly.

Repeat once, quickly.

The boats on the sea
Bob up and down,
Up and down,
Up and down.
The boats on the sea
Bob up and down,
Sailing on the ocean.

Loosen hands and bob up and down on the spot, matching movements to words.

The sailors on the boat
Climb up the mast,
Up the mast etc.

Mime climbing on the spot.

The flags on the boat
Fly flip, flip, flap,
Flip, flip, flap etc.

Flap one arm in front quickly.

The fish in the sea
Swim round and round,
Round and round etc.

Re-join hands and skip round in a circle.

Fun with Action Rhymes and Poems

Twinkle, Twinkle, Christmas Lights

Sing to the tune of ,Twinkle, Twinkle, Little Star'.

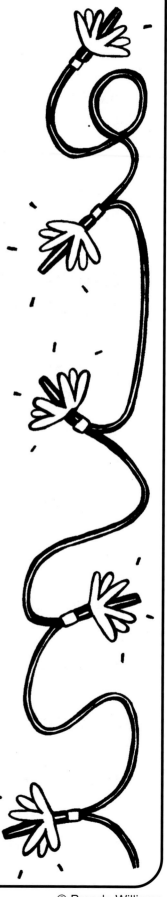

Twinkle, twinkle, Christmas lights.

Father Christmas came last night,

Up above the snowy skies,

Eating ice-cream and mince pies.

Twinkle, twinkle, Christmas lights,

Father Christmas came last night.

Twinkle, twinkle, Christmas tree,

Father Christmas came to me,

Down the chimney with the toys,

Woke me up with all his noise.

Twinkle, twinkle, Christmas snow,

Father Christmas, Ho! Ho! Ho!

Here's a Toy Box!

Sing to the tune of 'Frère Jacques'

Place a large mat in the centre of a circle of children.

Here's a toy box   *Point to mat.*
Here's a toy box

What's inside?   *Each child mimes lifting a lid in front of them.*
What's inside?

Tumble out, Teddy!   *All children gambol or roll.*
Tumble out, Teddy!

Teddy's here.   *One child is chosen to stand on the mat.*
Teddy's here.

Continue, suggesting other toys for other verses,
such as:
Hop along, Rabbit!   *Children make bunny hops and one is*
                              chosen to stand on mat.

And
Dance about, Dolly!

Leap about, Froggy!

Bounce about, Ball!

March around, Soldier!

Repeat from the beginning, returning all children from the mat back to the circle in turn.

Fun with Action Rhymes and Poems

The Horse Post

Sit the children in a circle and choose one child to be the postman galloping around the outside of the circle. At some point the postman silently drops a letter behind one of the children. At the end of the poem, the child who has the letter is the next postman.

Galloping, galloping,
    All day he rides
        Through all the towns
            And countryside.

Galloping, galloping,
    Bringing the post,
        From far and wide
            And coast to coast.

Galloping, galloping,
    People await
        At rich man's door
            And poor man's gate.

Galloping, galloping,
    Bringing the mail,
        Over the hills
            And over the dale.

Galloping, galloping,
    Maybe there'll be
        A letter for you,
            A letter for me.

Spider, Spider

A circle game

One child is chosen as a spider and the circle of children hold hands and lift them above the spider to form a web. A child chosen as a fly stands to one side.
Say the rhyme quietly and slowly till the last two lines.

Spinning a web   *Spider turns inside the circle.*
Is a spider, spider,
Carefully, carefully,   *Spider continues to turn slowly, as the circle of*
Wider, wider.   *children move slowly outwards still holding hands.*

In the web   *Spider sits in the centre.*
The spider, spider
Waits and waits,   *Fly quietly mimes flying around outside the circle.*
The web beside her.

Into the web   *Fly creeps into the circle on hands and knees.*
Of the spider, spider
Creeps a fly   *Fly creeps close to spider.*
Quite near beside her.

In the web
The spider, spider
Gives a GULP!   *Spider catches the fly by grabbing his shoulder.*
And the fly's inside her!

The fly is then the next spider!

Dawdling Dinosaurs

Invite one child to be Mum and stand to one side.

Danny the dinosaur

dawdled all day.

Children walk around with heavy 'dinosaur' steps, holding hands in front like claws.

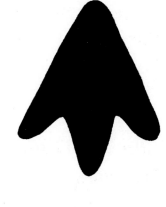

Dragging around

where dinosaurs play.

Drowsy and dozy,

Children lie down and pretend to sleep.

dreaming, he lay

Till Mum shouted 'Lunch time!'

Children kneel, ready to run.

Then, hey...........

Race to see who can touch Mum first.
Winner becomes next Mum.

He's away!

My Bear

Hold a real teddy bear and cuddle it each time the words 'My bear' are said.

I don't remember when he came.   *Shake head.*
My bear.

But he has always been the same.   *Look at bear.*
My bear.

Same black nose, same brown eyes,   *Touch bear's nose and eyes.*
Very quiet and very wise.
My bear.

He comes with me when I go far
And sits beside me in the car.   *Sit bear nearby.*
My bear.

He's in my bed when I go up
And seems to like to cuddle up.   *Pick up bear and cuddle it.*
My bear.

His eyes stay open all the night,   *Point to bear's eyes.*
He likes to see that I'm all right.   *Point to self.*
My bear.

And when the light is turned down
                                  low   *Hold bear to ear.*
I hear his heart beat very slow.
My bear.

We're special friends, a perfect pair,   *Hold bear up in front then cuddle it.*
He misses me when I'm not there.
My bear.

Fun with Action Rhymes and Poems

These Are My Special Things

A teddy in my bed at night.
    A torch, to beam the brightest light.

My scooter or my trike to ride.
    A secret place, where I can hide.

A splashy bath with bubbly foam.
    The ones I love, inside my home.

My little dog to run with me,
    And Granny, coming round to tea.

A holiday with sea and sun.
    A party, where we all have fun.

Storytime at nursery school,
    And feeding ducks around the pool.

My friends who come to play each day.
    I like these things a special way.

My Tiny Treasures

A sea shell.
A silver bell.

A shiny sweet.
A chocolate treat.

A jumping frog.
A tiny dog.

A special star.
A racing car.

A round bead, in brilliant blue.
A small and pretty dolly's shoe.

A golden ring.
Some yellow string.

A plastic rocket.
All

in my pocket!

My Grandma

I like the special way
my grandma smiles at me.
I like the special things
she makes me for my tea.

I like the special way
she listens when I talk.
I like the way she holds my hand
and takes me special walks.

I like the special way
my grandma reads me books.
And I like the special way
my special grandma looks.

Rainbow, Rainbow

Rainbow, rainbow
Sunny light
Shining through
The raindrops bright.

Red and yellow
Blue and green
Every colour
Ever seen.

Peacock's feather
Butterfly
Took their colours
From your sky.

Rainbow, rainbow
Come again
You're so lovely
After rain.

Fun with Action Rhymes and Poems

Winter Weather

Foggy day
We can't see
Hold on tight
Follow me!

Diamonds on
The window pane
Splashy walks
In the rain

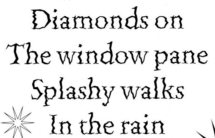

Hail falling
Hard and white
Stay inside
Hail can bite!

Skiddy roads
Ice in sheets
Slippy steps
Frozen feet

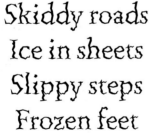

Silent world
Soft and white
Snow has fallen
In the night

The Wind Wizard

Can you hear the wind wizard   *Put hand to ear, listening.*

Whooshing through the trees?   *Rotate hands rapidly around each other.*

Weaving round the branches

Worrying the leaves?   *Stand, swaying body and waving arms.*

Can you hear the wind wizard   *Put hand to ear, listening.*

Whistling up high?   *Rotate hands rapidly around each other.*

Whipping up the storm clouds

Wheeling through the sky?   *Wave arms and hands above head.*

Can you hear the wind wizard   *Put hand to ear, listening.*

Whizzing up the lane?   *Rotate hands rapidly around each other.*

Whirling blossom in the air,   *Make scooping movements and fling arms high.*

Waltzing with the rain?   *Clasp hands in front, rock arms to mime waltzing.*

Can you see the wind wizard   *Place hands to eyes, looking up.*

When he whistles by?

Will you ever see him   *Shake head.*

In his wild, wild sky?

Fun with Action Rhymes and Poems

A Puddle Full of Raindrops

Stand in a circle.

A puddle full of raindrops
Makes a rainy day,
And I can splash in my big boots   *Stamp about, kicking feet up.*
To pass the time away!

A seaside full of sunshine
Means I can dig in sand,   *Mime digging.*
And run into the little waves
The sea pours on the land.   *Run forwards and backwards.*

A playground full of icy paths   *Mime sliding.*
And frosty patterned things
Brings spider's webs of snowy lace
Woven on the swings.   *Mime swinging.*

A garden full of snowflakes
To build a snowman tall.
I'll make deep footprints all around   *Walk round slowly and heavily.*
And roll a huge snowball!   *Mime rolling snow.*

A sky full of weather   *Point upwards.*
of rain or snow or sun,
No matter what the weather
We'll have days full of fun!   *Hold hands and skip in a circle.*

Puddles

Big puddles,
Small puddles,
Puddles in the lane.
Puddles on the footpath,
Puddles near the drain.

Shiny puddles,
Muddy puddles,
Puddles that grow.
Winter puddles,
Icy puddles,
Puddles of snow.

Spring puddles,
Summer puddles,
Puddles on the grass.
Squashy puddles,
Sploshy puddles,
Puddles to......**splash!**

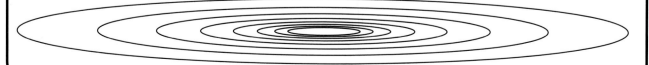

Fun with Action Rhymes and Poems

Title Index

A Fruit to Suit?	69	Mini-beasts	36
A Puddle Full of Raindrops	106	My Bear	99
About Time!	50	My Grandma	102
All Is Quiet	38	My Hands, My Feet	27
Am I the Tallest?	59	My House	73
Apple Bobbing	64	My Tiny Treasures	101
Autumn's Here	86	New Life	87
Candles for Hanukkah	61	Night and Day Shapes	91
Caterpillar, Caterpillar	37	One Little Monkey	48
Changing Sands	40	Over the Sea	56
Chocolate	68	Painting Pictures	44
Clouds	39	Patterns on the Sand	84
Colours Here and Colours There	45	Puddles	107
Countdown to Bedtime	49	Rainbow, Rainbow	103
Dawdling Dinosaurs	98	Rapping in the Jungle	32
Day and Night	54	Sailing on the Ocean	93
Dear Potato	70	Scuttling Spider	71
Down in the Jungle	47	Shape that Dough	90
Drawing Shapes	92	Show Five Fingers	28
Eid Mubarak (Happy Eid)	60	Spider, Spider	97
Family Barbecue	55	Spider, Spider Spinning Well	34
Family Lunch	57	Stepping Through the Day	51
Farm Journey	76	The Chip Shop Man	83
Farmer, Farmer	81	The Doctor	80
Finger Farm	33	The Dragon Dance	63
Finger Teddies	46	The Horse Post	96
Gloves	29	The Market	65
Here's a Toy Box	95	The Mehndi Tree	43
I'm the Butcher	66	The Scarecrow	85
I've Made a Star	62	The Train Journey	75
I Can Do Opposites	26	The Wind Wizard	105
I Can Make Noises	30	There Goes the Train	79
I Have a Baby Sister	58	These Are My Special Things	100
I Love Bread	67	Travelling	77
In Granny's Garden	72	Twinkle, Twinkle Christmas Lights	94
Jack Frost	88	When I Was Born	41
Jungle Wood	35	When Night Comes	53
Just a Taste	31	When the Sun Steals Away	52
Let's Climb up a Rainbow	42	Who am I?	82
Look at Shapes	89	Winter Weather	104
Magic Carpet	78		
Make the Bed	74		